Including Children w Asperger's Syndrome in the Early Years Foundation Stage

Written by
Clare Beswick

Illustrated by
Martha Hardy

Published 2010 by A&C Black Publishers Limited
36 Soho Square, London W1D 3QY
www.acblack.com

ISBN 978-1408-129-48-7

First published in the UK by Featherstone Education 2005 (Updated 2007)
Text © Clare Beswick 2005
Illustrations © Martha Hardy

Printed in Great Britain by Latimer Trend & Company Limited.

This book is produced using paper that is made from wood grown in
managed, sustainable forests. It is natural, renewable and recyclable.
The logging and manufacturing processes conform to the environmental
regulations of the country of origin.

**To see our full range of titles
visit www.acblack.com**

Contents

Introduction

Imagination, creativity, exploration, discovery, play, communication and social interaction are all at the heart of the Early Years Foundation Stage.

The busy, constantly changing and developing, visually stimulating and socially demanding worlds created in early years settings are ideally placed to enable young children to learn. However, the freedom and flexibility of provision, the wealth of choice and self-determined activity in the Early Years Foundation Stage is uniquely challenging for children with autistic spectrum disorders, including Asperger's Syndrome. With energy, determination and imagination children with Asperger's can thrive in the Early Years Foundation Stage.

This book is here to help you to adapt your practice to help young children with Asperger's Syndrome gain the most from their Early Years Foundation Stage experience. It aims to inform, encourage and reassure you. Early years practitioners are experts in early childhood and have a unique opportunity to really get to know and tune into individual children. The skills, experience and insight gained as an early years practitioner are just what you need to make inclusion really work for all children in your setting.

This book will:

Inform you by:

- providing essential background information to get you started;
- telling you about the implications of Asperger's Syndrome for learning across the areas of learning in the Early Years Foundation Stage;
- giving information about some different approaches or ways of working and what we can learn from them;
- introducing the multi-agency team;
- signposting you to further resources.

Support you by:

- managing the routines of everyday;
- giving tried and tested teaching tips;
- planning the environment and organisation;
- giving ideas and activities using everyday resources;
- giving practical ideas for differentiation.

Make you think by asking:
- how might it feel to have Asperger's?
- what's it like to feel different?
- what is it like to parent a child with special needs?
- how you could help other staff and children understand

Make you ask yourself some hard questions such as:
- how can I make real connections with this child?
- how can I use this child's strengths to best advantage?
- how can I help this child's self esteem and build friendships?
- how can I help everyone to understand, value and support all children in the setting?

Who is this book for?

This book is for anyone with a real interest in very young children with autistic spectrum disorders, students and early years practitioners. Many of the practical ideas and suggestions can be easily adapted for children of different ages with communication difficulties, working at this developmental stage.

Make you ask yourself some hard questions such as:
- easy-to-do ideas, using everyday resources;
- activities planned specifically for children with Asperger's Syndrome;
- links with the stepping stones in the early years curriculum guidance for the Early Years Foundation Stage;
- lots of opportunity for small-step learning, repetition and reinforcement;
- careful reflection of the implications of Asperger's Syndrome on learning;
- ideas on organisation, structure and routines.

Making the most of this book

Read the first pages of this book for an overview of Asperger's Syndrome. Then spend time observing the child in different situations, with different people. A little background knowledge will ensure that you understand the implications of what you observe.

- Listen to the parents' view of their child and encourage them to tell you about their aspirations and their fears.
- Read on for more information about the implications of Asperger's syndrome for learning.
- Look at the pages for each area of learning for ideas and tips to make sure all the activities offered in the setting are accessible to the child with special needs.
- Think about the routines, structures and demands of the child's day and consider the implications of their special needs.
- Check out the pages on different approaches and multi-agency working for more information and signposting to further resources.

This book aims to be a practical resource. Keep it handy and dip into it for ideas and inspiration. Every child with Asperger's Syndrome is different, but pass this book around the team so that everyone has an insight into autism and what this means for the child as an individual, the other children and the setting as a whole.

What is Asperger's Syndrome?

Asperger's Syndrome is a neurological disorder named after Austrian pediatrician Hans Asperger, who in 1944 described a pattern of behaviour in several young boys who had normal intelligence and language development, but also had several autistic-like behaviours as well as social and communication difficulties. However, the term Asperger's Syndrome only came into use following research published by Lorna Wing in 1981, which recognised Asperger's Syndrome as a unique disorder.

Asperger's Syndrome is part of a wider group of disorders called autistic spectrum disorders. Autism is a disorder that affects the way a person communicates and interacts with other people. Most people with autism also have learning difficulties, but people with Asperger's Syndrome have average or above average intelligence.

"In order for learning to take place, children's bodies must take part in physical experience."
(Rhythms of Learning, Brewer and Campbell).

"Good outcomes for children are linked to adult-child interactions which involve sustained shared thinking and open ended questioning."
(EPPE Project, DCFS).

What do we know about he differences between girls and boys?

From birth, boys and girls are different and their brains develop in different ways. When a baby is born, he or she has made relatively few links between the two hemispheres or sides of the brain. As soon as babies are born, and in response to each experience, they begin to build on these links, making more dendrites (connections) between the neurons in their brains.

Nutrition, stimulation, touch, taste, smell, hearing all contribute to the process, and the richer the environment the faster the baby will make the links. From as early as six weeks, boys will tend to concentrate on developing the right half of their brain (the half that deals with objects) while girls tend to concentrate on the left half (the half that deals with faces and sounds). Experienced practitioners will know that when children enter their setting, girls are still generally more interested in people and how they work, boys are still more interested in things and how they work.

We now have evidence that girls will usually choose activities that involve (or are near) an adult. Girls watch adults closely and model their behaviour. In role play, girls are likely to imitate adults (their mothers, older siblings, and the practitioners in the setting). It is girls who invent games about doing the register, organising snack and mealtimes, going shopping, cleaning up. Their play is often uncannily accurate, and we sometimes see and hear ourselves repeated in embarrassing accuracy by the girls we work with!

Most girls have made sufficient links in their brains to begin the complex skills of reading and writing by the time they are four and a half, while in most boys it is nearer six. We need to use this knowledge as we work.

Before a child can learn the complex skills of reading and writing, they need to make hundreds of thousands of links between their left brain and right brain, through the 'super highway' of the brain called the corpus callosum.

Getting started

Every child is different and will be affected by Asperger's differently. They will also be very much affected by the people around them, the way they interact and behave with them, their environment and the routines and experiences at home and in other familiar places.

Asperger's, Able Autism and the Continuum

Asperger's Syndrome is an autistic spectrum disorder. That is, it is part of the autistic continuum, where every individual has a differing degree of autism and varying intelligence level. Many people consider Asperger's Syndrome to refer to those children with fewer autistic traits and average or above average intelligence. However, there are different views on this.

Some researchers believe there are differences between able autism and Asperger's, others believe the differences are not significant. Some of the brightest children most mildly affected with Asperger's Syndrome may remain undiagnosed but appear odd or eccentric.

As every child is an individual, and each child with Asperger's is an individual and will function differently in every setting, the distinction is perhaps not something to get too concerned about. Concentrate instead on each child's individual learning style, strengths and needs.

How can you help?

There is much that can be done to help young children with Asperger's within early years settings and at home. The key is to understand the way the child thinks and perceives the world. Careful observation, planned intervention and listening to parents can provide some insight. By developing our abilities to see the world from the child's viewpoint, we can be most effective in helping that child.

There is also much we can learn from approaches developed to address the needs of children with autistic spectrum disorders. We can learn from these approaches and adapt them to help us meet the needs of the child within the busy early years setting.

When you work with children with speech and language delay, it is useful to think of praise, prompts and rewards as essential tools.

Support needs to:

- be consistent;

- focus on developing the child's communication skills;

- develop the child's awareness of others and build social skills;

- use special interests and skills to best advantage;

- promote the child's friendships;

- build self esteem, insight and self knowledge.

Stage and Play

Children with Asperger's Syndrome often find the busy, stimulating world of their early years setting a confusing and difficult place. Early years settings are highly sociable worlds, with a constant to and fro between individual children, groups of children and adults. Each social interaction has a different set of rules and requires children to have empathy, an awareness of others and the needs of others, and an emerging understanding of not just words, but body language, facial expression, humour and metaphor.

Most children of four and five years of age are effective communicators, with an amazing grasp of the more subtle aspects of language and social interaction. Children with Asperger's are not easily sociable beings.

They tend to have difficulty with:

- interpreting what is said because they take requests such as 'Go and wash your hands in the toilet' very literally;

- nicknames and shortened names – Joseph and Joe – are they two children or the same child?

- sayings, such as 'Over the top', 'Second thoughts', or 'Raining cats and dogs';

- words with more than one meaning, such as jumper or cool;

- vagaries, such as maybe or perhaps;

- jokes and plays on words;

- social timing;

- knowing when to talk and when to listen;

- knowing when the other child is interested in what they have to say;

- saying or asking the same thing over and over and over again.

Play in the Early Years Foundation Stage pivots on young children's:

- social interaction and communication;

- shared understanding;

- common interests;

- drive to explore, experiment and discover;

- rich imaginative worlds;

- desire to be part of the group;

- need to build friendships.

Many children with Asperger's, like other children with autistic spectrum disorders, prefer sameness and routine, actively avoid new and confusing experiences, do not have the same interests as other young children, and have little understanding that others do not share their own special interests. This, together with difficulties with empathy and social understanding, makes complex, imaginative group play an alien environment for any children with Asperger's.

To help children with Asperger's develop play skills, practitioners can:

- model simple pretend play;

- use routine and more structured play as a gateway;

- start with the child's own special interests and encourage more flexible ways of playing with the child's special objects, such as introducing bus timetables to the home corner or outside play area;

- be mindful of the child's sensitivities to particular stimuli, such as the feel of dressing up clothes, the texture or smell of the sand, the shadows in the outside play area and so on.

Using routines

Routines are an effective way of helping the child with Asperger's to make sense of their environment, the session and social conventions within the setting. Routines can be fixed sequences of interaction or an order of events.

Effective routines have:

- a clear purpose;

- picture, photo, action or symbol clues as reinforcers, prompts or reminders;

- a clear beginning and a definite end;

and are

- used consistently across the setting by all practitioners, as well as consistently between home and school.

Use routines to give clear signals, clarify messages and teach conventions. They build understanding and help the child with Asperger's fit into friendship groups. Get started on using routine to:

- greet or register the children each day; in the same way

- make a photo timetable of activities or events for the day

- use a song or chant to comment on what is happening, such as when the children are getting ready to go out to play, such as,

'Toys away, coats on, ready to play outside

Toys away, coats on, ready to play outside

Let's go!'

Sensory issues

Many adults with autistic spectrum disorders, including Asperger's Syndrome report feelings of huge distress caused by ordinary everyday sensations which we are hardly aware of, such as the hum and flicker of fluorescent lighting or the feel of clothes and shoes. Some noises, such as that of the vacuum cleaner or washing machine, are too loud or almost painful.

Smells can also be an issue, with children being distressed or fascinated by particular odours or aromas.

Personal accounts written by people with Asperger's Syndrome are filled with references to sensory experiences, and many refer to these being at the most intense during childhood. Over time, children learn to cope with these sensory experiences and find strategies for living with them.

Observation, tuning into the individual child with Asperger's and listening to parents are the only ways to identify such sensory issues. Sometimes it is obvious, such as the child who sits with their fingers in their ears, or folds over their outer ear, but it can be more difficult to pinpoint. A child who hates travelling on a bus may be anxious because they could be not knowing where they are going, the motion of the bus, the lights or the texture of the seat could also affect them.

Early years practitioners can help within settings by:

- raising awareness of sensory issues with other staff;

- removing unnecessary noise;

- providing a comfortable safe haven;

- looking out for sensations that might be distressing the child;

- trying to tune in and see the world from the child's perspective;

- talking and listening to the child, giving them a chance to tell you how they are feeling through words, drawings and play.

Getting your message across

With very literal understanding, sensory issues and difficulties with abstract thinking, sometimes getting the message across and being sure of genuine understanding can be a challenge for the early years practitioner working with a child with Asperger's in their setting.

Ways to help include:

- speaking in concrete and real terms;

- being descriptive in praise, such as saying 'you kept trying and then you got the brick in the right place – well done' instead of just 'well done';

- avoiding sensory overload, removing unnecessary background noise;

- starting with the child's name – they need to know you are talking to them;

- using small steps and bite-size chunks to convey information;

- using pictures and photographs as visual clues;

- presenting information visually, clearly and consistently.

Building friendships

As children start to play alongside and then with small groups of friends, they begin to find other children with common interests and children that they enjoy playing with. Children begin to make the first tentative steps towards particular friends that they choose for themselves, as opposed to the children that they live close to, or the children of their parent's friends.

These emerging friendships depend on:

- shared attention;

- common interest;

- play and imagination;

- empathy;

- social understanding.

These are all things with which many children with Asperger's Syndrome struggle.

The early years is the ideal time to develop strategies for helping the child with Asperger's to understand others and build friendships. It is also the time to start building the other children's understanding and respect for all children, irrespective of difference.

Check out the pages on communication and personal social and emotional development for ideas, but to get you started:

- practice turn taking with simple fun games;

- try to build their special interests into other games;

- teach by modelling and simple pretend play – it helps the child with Asperger's Syndrome get involved in home corner and other play;

- when playing games that involve teams, give the child with Asperger's the chance to choose a partner, or arrange the pairs yourself, but avoid the child being last to have a partner;

- keep instructions and explanations simple, concrete and real;

- try to teach social skills in real situations;

- take nothing for granted; explain what is required clearly and in small chunks;

- teach social conventions, they oil the wheels of friendship.

A fish out of water?

Personal accounts of what it feels like to have Asperger's Syndrome abound. Each is different and all are incredibly moving, but without doubt they also provide us with a window or at least a glimpse into the way some children and adults with Asperger's think, learn and perceive the world.

Almost without exception, adults with Asperger's describe themselves as being fundamentally different, as thinking differently, and experiencing the world differently. The challenge for early years practitioners is not just to help the child with Asperger's to make sense of the world, but to help other children to accept and celebrate differences of all kinds.

Reading accounts of able people with autistic spectrum disorders provides invaluable insight. Try Donna Williams' widely available biography 'Inside Out', or the fictional story 'The Curious Incident of the Dog in the Night Time'. See page 47–48 for other information, including websites prepared by adults and children with Asperger's Syndrome.

The other side of the fence

For parents, getting a diagnosis is likely to be time consuming, difficult and stressful. They may have had vague concerns about their child not fitting in, or appearing odd for some time, and in some instances despite the shock and confirmation that their child is different, a diagnosis can also be a relief.

Every parent reacts differently to both the assessment process and a diagnosis. But, almost universally, parents report a mixture of feelings of shock, disbelief, anger and guilt. Some parents seek out information and resources, others need time to absorb and think about their child and this life changing information.

The challenge for those working with the child is to offer support that is sensitive to the ever-changing needs of the parents and wider family in this time of great change and stress.

Practitioners can help by ensuring they:

- are well informed;

- have information available for all staff in the setting;

- know where they can go for information;

- are positive, reassuring and determined;

- are organised and focused in their planning of how they will meet the child's needs;

- regularly provide honest but positive feedback to parents about their child;

- are committed to and make time for multi-agency working.

Working together to meet the needs of their child will give parents:
- confidence and hope;
- greater insight;
- knowledge, tips and ideas.

It will also allow them to:
- share the anxiety;
- enjoy their child.

Early years practitioners have the skills and experience to work effectively with all parents, and particularly parents under stress. Having learnt a little about this most complex of disorders and begun to see how autism is expressed in a particular child, further insight can be gained by trying to imagine how the world might seem to that child. You can do this by listening to parents and really watching their child, trying to tune into their interactions and communications, and thinking about how they respond to different situations and people.

Personal accounts written by older children and adults with autism and Asperger's Syndrome give a unique insight into how the world might seem to the child with autism. Although each account is very personal and highly individual, common themes do emerge as adults reflect on their early childhood experiences. There are many personal accounts and you can find links to further resources through the website of the National Autistic Society.

Children with Asperger's Syndrome and the six areas of learning

Children with Asperger's Syndrome have average or above average intelligence but have difficulties with communication, social interaction, abstract thinking and organisation, as well as repetitive special interests that can get in the way of learning and socialising.

They will have more difficulty with some of the EYFS six areas of learning than others, and although each child will be affected differently, there is much that early years practitioners can do to help each child across the six areas of learning.

In the following pages, we explore each of the areas of learning, and make suggestions on the following:

- the implications for learning in that area;

- the particular stepping stones in the Foundation Curriculum, which may prove to be challenging;

- some ideas and activities to try;

- top tips for success in that area of learning.

Personal, social and emotional development

Personal, social and emotional development is at the heart of the EYFS, enabling children to become effective learners, have a positive sense of self and establish successful relationships with other children and adults.

What's different for the child with Asperger's Syndrome?

- Children with Asperger's Syndrome have difficulty understanding the social interactions that are the basis of communication and friendships. They may have lots of speech, but it is the way they use this speech and understand the language of others that causes difficulties.

- They often have difficulty understanding the needs of others, and that others may have a different perspective or point of view. They will rarely understand that others do not share their special or repetitive interests, and this often gets in the way of developing friendships.

- Humour and the sharing confidences or experiences oil the wheels of developing friendships and social interactions. These are very difficult for many children with Asperger's.

- Children with Asperger's often want to be part of the group, having a need for others, and are distressed by the difficulties they encounter. This can lead to difficulties with confidence and self esteem, causing the child and parents significant distress.

- Shared attention, when children talking or playing together share a common interest or purpose, is difficult for children with Asperger's. They need to be specifically taught and shown the social rules that other children learn instinctively.

- Sensory issues (the way they process and experience sensory inputs) can cause considerable distraction and get in the way of attention and listening skills.

- Children with Asperger's Syndrome, like other children with autistic spectrum disorders, prefer their lives to be ordered and constant. They do not seek out new experiences, or initiate new ideas that have the potential to add to their innate confusion and difficulty in understanding the world.

Asperger's Syndrome, Personal Social and Emotional Development and the EYFS Guidance

Children with Asperger's will need particular help to:

- Develop a curiosity about things and processes; have a positive approach to new experiences; take pleasure in learning new skills.

- Display high levels of involvement in activities.

- Have a developing awareness of their own needs, views and feelings and be sensitive to the needs, views and feelings of others.

- Feel safe and secure and demonstrate a sense of trust; seek out others to share experiences; relate and make attachments to members of their group.

- Work as part of a group, or class, taking turns and sharing fairly, understanding that there need to be agreed values and codes of behaviour for groups of people, including adults and children, to work together harmoniously.

- Consider the consequences of their words and actions for themselves and others.

Ideas and activities to try

- Practise lots of simple turn taking games, with one or two other children. Give clear and concise instructions and make the games fun and easy to do. They could blow lots of bubbles and take turns to jump up and pop one, take turns to bowl balls at skittles or take turns to add bricks to a tower and so on.

- Look together at simple photographs of people. Talk together about what the people are doing, how they are feeling and how we know what they are feeling.

- Join in simple pretend play one to one or in small groups, modelling and explaining words to describe feelings and emotions, such as 'tired', 'happy' and so on.

Top Tips

- Be very positive about the child's special interests, at the same time as agreeing clear and consistent rules for their enjoyment. For a child with a fascination for car registration numbers, it is okay for them to ask staff for their car numbers once at the beginning of each session, but not to ask all the parents every day. In this instance, this would need to go alongside teaching other social conventions, such as how to greet people, and joining in with others' chat, by talking about what they are talking about.

- Try to model these social rules in real life and simple pretend play of everyday situations of importance to the child.

- Provide lots of praise and positive comments that are specific and descriptive.

- Think about the people in the child's life. Discuss what you plan and do with the child's parents, and plan together opportunities for home and the setting to increase the number and scope of the child's friends.

Circles of Friends

'Circles of Friends' is a tool for inclusion that developed in the USA, but is successfully used in schools with older children in the UK. It involves the child's peers providing support on a day-to-day basis to widen and develop the child's circle of friends in a planned and informed way. It is helpful for early years practitioners to be aware of the principles and processes of Circles of Friends as there is much of the philosophy that can be of great benefit to all children within the early years setting.

Find out more at: **www.inclusion.com** and **www.inclusive-solutions.com**

Communication, language and literacy

Effective communication is so much more than words and recognising letters. It is an essential building block not only for children's future learning but also for social interaction, being part of a group, co-operative play, teams and friendships. The child with Asperger's Syndrome may have unique strengths in some parts of this area of learning, such as the recognition of print and visual discrimination, but will have unique difficulties in other parts, particularly the more subtle aspects of communication and social interaction.

What's different for the child with Asperger's Syndrome?

- A strong visual learning style will for many children make recognising letters and words in print easier and indeed may be a useful way to begin building spoken language skills.

- Children with Asperger's are likely to have difficulties with conversation and shared attention, making interacting and negotiating with others more difficult.

- Understanding tends to be and remain very literal, which makes jokes, humour and nonsense play with words confusing. Life needs to be fun, so all this is best not avoided but explained!

- All children in the Early Years Foundation Stage learn best through practical experience and exploring everyday objects and situations. Children with Asperger's Syndrome tend to have particular and ongoing difficulties with abstract thinking and concepts.

- Some children with Asperger's can focus and attend extraordinarily well on their special interest or an activity of their own choice. However, attention to other activities may be much more limited. Many children with Asperger's can focus on only one piece of information at a time, known as centration. They have difficulty attending to several elements of the same task at the same time. A small steps approach to tasks, breaking activities into separate chunks or parts is often helpful, as well as removing unnecessary elements and distractions.

- Mark making may be difficult, as many children with Asperger's Syndrome have co-ordination difficulties, which may make them appear somewhat clumsy or uncoordinated.

Asperger's Syndrome, Communication, Language and Literacy and the EYFS Guidance

Children with Asperger's will need particular help to:

- Initiate conversation, attend to and take account of what others say, and use talk to resolve agreements

- Interact with others, negotiating plans and activities and taking turns in conversation

- Use language to imagine and recreate roles and experiences

- Enjoy rhyming and rhythmic activities, continue a rhyming string; recognise rhythm in spoken words

Ideas and activities to try

- Practice making choices and taking turns at every opportunity.

- Use rote learning and memory strengths to teach recognition of letters and words in print. These can then be used to provide excellent prompts to understanding concepts and new ideas.

- Try lots of different mark makers and mark-making play and activities.

- Try passing actions or sounds around a small circle of children, each child copying an action from the child next to them, and then making the sameaction for the child on the other side of them to copy.

- Play lots of clapping and rhythm games, copying actions and rhythm patterns.

- Choose listening games to build attention and concentration, using visual prompts to help.

- Create a scrapbook together of pictures and words around the child's special interests and favourite toys and games. Use looking at this as a reward and a relaxing time for the child.

- Provide visual clues and prompts to help understanding

- Use routine to help children develop organisational skills and make sense of their day.

- Make comments, questions, praise and instructions short, accurate and descriptive, such as '*Name* you fastened the zip yourself, well done'.

- Use the child's name first to capture their attention, and so that they know they need to attend to what you are saying.

- Break information down into small bite size chunks. Concentrating can be hard in such a confusing world, particularly if they are many conflicting sensory experiences and distractions for the child.

- Beware of clutter! Try to remove unnecessary distractions, turn off background noises, clear surfaces of clutter and so on. They compete for attention and can be more distracting to the child with Asperger's than to other children at a similar developmental stage.

- Try to limit choices. Too much choice is overly confusing and distracting.

- Sometimes singing instructions helps the child to attend and tune in to what is being said.

Problem solving, reasoning and numeracy

Children need to be confident in a whole range of key skills and have opportunity to develop their mathematical understanding through a range of play, activities and experiences. In the Early Years Foundation Stage children need to learn about number, counting, sorting and matching, patterns and connections, about shapes, space and measures. Children begin to learn about concepts such as size, space and time and to make generalisations, estimations and predictions based on their knowledge and understanding.

What's different for the child with Asperger's Syndrome?

- Children with Asperger's Syndrome may have good or exceptional rote memory skills, particularly for facts, numbers, dates, times, ages, etc.

- They tend to like order and predictability and can often, given time, excel at mathematical development and similar subjects.

- Difficulties with abstract thinking and concepts need to be considered, with activities being presented with visual prompts, and in concrete real terms. As with all young children, those with Asperger's need to learn by doing, and may have difficulty generalising the concepts and ideas they have learnt.

- Some children with Asperger's have a particular talent for the computer! This can be used very successfully to teach mathematical and other concepts.

Asperger's Syndrome, Problem Solving, Reasoning and Numeracy and the EYFS Guidance

Children with Asperger's may need particular help with abstract thinking and concepts, such as:

- Use developing mathematical ideas and methods to solve practical problems

- Find items from positional or directional clues

- Show an awareness of symmetry

A visual learning style, strengths in rote learning and a delight in order may make numbers, ordering and counting easier for some children with Asperger's.

Ideas and activities to try

- Play lots of domino and number lotto games to practice turn taking, as well as counting and number recognition.

- Play number line games in pairs and small groups of children.

- Use number rhymes and action songs to help the child develop a deeper understanding of mathematical language.

- Use everyday objects to explore size and shape. Make the learning as real and concrete as possible, such as feeling and exploring everyday round objects, rather than making patterns with round shapes.

- Use sorting and matching skills to build simple pretend play, such as washing and sorting toy cutlery in the home corner or matching and sorting pairs of socks.

- Practice mathematical ideas and language in real everyday situations, when the child has to learn to use their mathematical knowledge in social situations, such as a trip to the shops.

Top Tips

- Children will need lots of encouragement to try out new ideas.

- Use the child's memory and rote learning strengths, but always check that the child understands what they have learnt and can generalise it. For example that child who can recognise the numeral three understands that represents three objects, and can recognise this numeral in different prints, places and situations, such as on a house door, in a book or on the birthday chart.

- Encourage the child to work with a partner when using the computer or other ICT equipment.

- Consider the way you present the materials, removing distractions and ambiguities, as well as planning for visual prompts.

- Use a child's special interests to work towards mathematical goals. For a child with a special interest in trains, fix small labels with numerals on, one to each coach, and play at matching, sorting, selecting, naming and ordering. For a child with a special interest in a particular colour, say green, practice making patterns with different green objects, look for green objects of different shapes, sort and match green objects.

Knowledge and understanding of the world

Young children generally have an innate desire to explore and investigate aspects of their world. As their confidence and experiences grow, they push back the boundaries, exploring and discovering far beyond their everyday experience. They thrive on firsthand experiences, observing, gathering information, using all their senses, doing, trying out new ideas and practising new skills. They explore new ideas. These processes and experiences form the foundation for their future learning in science, history, geography, design and technology as well as information and communication technology.

What's different for the child with Asperger's Syndrome?

- Children with autistic spectrum disorders, including Asperger's Syndrome, are not driven instinctively to explore their world. Often the world is a confusing and unpredictable place, particularly for those with sensory integration difficulties, quite understandably, do not actively seek to explore, discover, investigate and make sense of their world.

- Special interests can often be narrow and very focused, and for many children with Asperger's these special interests are their comfort zone and they will resist attempts by others to widen their interests.

- Children with Asperger's often have difficulty with abstract concepts and need to have materials and new ideas presented visually and learn through doing.

- Investigation of our world often depends on our abilities to interact with others and explore and question issues of difference, such as gender, culture, ethnicity and religion. Children with Asperger's have difficulties with this higher level of interaction and understanding of others' needs and viewpoints.

- Perseverance, when a child gets stuck on a particular idea, can be an issue. Distracting the child rarely works, but is worth a try. More usefully, the practitioner needs to reflect on why the child is stuck. Is this a response to a particularly stressful situation, related to sensory inputs the child is experiencing, or simply the child's mindset of the moment? Ignoring usually works in the end, but may require an iron will, absolute consistency and the support of other staff.

- Children may be unusually sensitive or desensitised to certain sensory experiences, such as different textures, smells, the feel of water and so on.
Listening to parents and observing will help practitioners identify any sensory issues. This impacts on much of the sensory play activities of this area of learning.

Asperger's Syndrome, Knowledge and Understanding of the World and the EYFS Guidance

Children with Asperger's may need particular help to:

- Show curiosity and interest by facial expression, movement and sound; show curiosity, observe and manipulate objects; investigate objects and materials using all their senses as appropriate

- Show an interest in why things happen and how things work

- Build and construct with a wide range of objects; selecting appropriate resources, and adapting their work as necessary

- Show an interest in the lives of people familiar to them; find out about past and present events in their own lives, and in those of their families and other people they know

- Gain an awareness of the cultures and beliefs of others; begin to know about their own cultures and beliefs and those of other people

Ideas and activities to try

- For children who enjoy ICT activities, use strengths and interest in collecting data as a reward, for example, using the roamer with a partner.

- Use step-by-step picture or photo instructions to prompt the child to explore different activities. Talk about the different ways they might explore materials and activities.

- Put together a treasure basket of different textures and observe the child's response to the range of materials.

- Take photographs of activities and everyday situations and use these to prompt the child.

- Start with everyday situations that the child is comfortable with, such as going to the park, and then plan new sensory and exploring activities, such as collecting leaves, twigs and other materials and seeing how they float can be used to make patterns and shapes.

- Make the best use of ICT to encourage the child to explore and discover, by gathering information, printing, scanning and taking photos.

- Create a visual diary using photos, pictures and objects to explain to the child what is going to happen when going out and about, or trying new experiences.

- Be mindful of sensory issues and be flexible and practical in response. If a child hates the smell or feel of play dough, try adding different oils or essences to change the aroma, try different colours of dough, try dough that is more or less sticky, try using dough with clean dough tools, try salt dough, selfhardening dough or clay.

- Plan activities so children can get involved and respond and record their observations in a range of ways, including non-verbal means.

- Introduce new experiences slowly and step by step.

- When using open-ended questions to encourage children to predict or consider, try to use language that is clear, concise and unambiguous.

- Exploring and being aware of change is very much a part of knowledge and understanding of the world in the Early Years Foundation Stage. Be sensitive to the fact that change is the last thing that most children with Asperger's want to experience and maybe even observe. Help the child by using photos and clear concise phrases to explain changes and offer reassurance.

Physical development

Moving with confidence, control and co-ordination, and manipulating objects small and large with skill and accuracy are central to physical development in the early years curriculum. They give children the ability to enjoy physical activity and active play, as well as feel the positive benefits of exercise and physical activity.

What's different for the child with Asperger's Syndrome?

- Many children with Asperger's Syndrome have difficulties with co-ordination.

- Sensory integration difficulties can also impact on how children develop motor skills.

- A competitive spirit and the need to bepart of a group often motivate children. Motivation is often an issue for children with Asperger's who may need much encouragement and meaningful rewards.

- Active groups and team games are difficult as they are based on common understanding and shared goals – something with which many children with Asperger's struggle.

- Outside play is full of unexpected noises, sounds, sights, smells and movement. All this extra sensory input can be confusing.

- Some children with Asperger's have considerable difficulty learning to pedal. Make sure that 'sit-and-ride' trundle toys of the right size are available for the child.

Asperger's Syndrome, Physical Development and the EYFS Guidance

Children with Asperger's may need particular help to:
- Negotiate space successfully when playing racing and chasing games with other children; show awareness of space, of themselves and others

- Move with confidence, imagination and safety; move with control and co-ordination

- Initiate new combinations of movement and gesture in order to express and respond to feelings, ideas and experiences

- Collaborate in devising and sharing tasks, including those which involve accepting rules

- Using increasing control over an object by touching, pushing, patting, throwing, catching and kicking it

- Handle tools, objects, construction and malleable materials safely and with increasing control

Ideas and activities to try

- Draw a shape on the floor and take turns with other children to step/jump/hop in and out of the circle.

- Play lots of throwing and target games, rolling and throwing balls, quoits, sponges, and bean bags and so on at different targets. Make the target area very bright and strongly contrasting to the background, such as a yellow bucket on a black background.

- Play 'Follow my leader', practising imitating actions and being part of a group.

- Try lots of clapping and stamping games, particularly those that involve two children or an adult and the child working together. Remember those traditional playground hand clapping games when you clapped hands with your partner across the mid-line (your right hand clapping your partner's right hand as they face you).

- Rowing and rocking action songs and games are great to build interaction between two children and require children to show awareness of the needs of their partner.

- Hold the child's hands as they sit and bounce up and down on either a small trampoline or large bouncy ball. Try stopping and starting to music, or counting ten bounces and then stop, and so on.

- Make simple stepping stones with chalk and practice balancing and stepping. Chalk lines, straight, curving, squiggly to balance along.

Top Tips

- Be mindful of any new smells, sounds, or changes in outside play, such as the feel of the wind or the noise of a lawnmower and so on.

- Make sure that the child with Asperger's Syndrome has a partner early on, when pairing children up for group games. Imagine trying to fit in, feeling different and then being last to have a partner.

- Try and build simple pretend play into outdoor play, as well as imitating everyday chores, such as wiping down surfaces, watering plants, sweeping leaves and so on.

- Look out for wheeled toys that carry more than one child, such as trolleys and trailers.

- Mark the edge of steps with brightly coloured paint.

Art, music, dance, role-play and imaginative play are all key elements of creative development in the Foundation Stage. They provide opportunities for children to express their emotions, encounter and explore new situations and feelings in a safe way and to build friendships. Such creativity gives young children a freedom and voice to explore and express feelings and emotions that they may not necessarily understand. It creates bridges and connections between different areas of learning and development

What's different for the child with Asperger's Syndrome?

- Many children with Asperger's Syndrome seek order and organisation to help them make sense of the world. They prefer limited repetitive and narrow interests to exploring and reaching out to new experiences and emotions.

- Motivation and curiosity are natural instincts for many children with Asperger's.

- Sensory issues can impact on children's early art experiences.

- Some children and adults with Asperger's and other autistic spectrum disorders have exceptional artistic talent and use painting and sculpture as a way of expressing themselves, or representing and making sense of the world. Look out for the work of Donna Williams and Stephen Derbyshire.

- Imaginative play, where one object or action represents another, depends on symbolic understanding, empathy and a wide range of social interaction skills. Many children with Asperger's find this very difficult, struggling to understand the real everyday concrete world, never mind the rich and varied world of the imagination.

Asperger's Syndrome, Physical Development and the EYFS Guidance

Children with Asperger's may need particular help to:
- use their bodies to explore texture and space; explore colour, texture, shape, form and space in two or three dimensions

- pretend that one object represents another; use available resources to create props to support role-play; play co-operatively as part of a group to act out a narrative; use their imagination, in art and design, music, dance, imaginative and role play stories

- express and communicate their ideas, thoughts and feelings by using a widening range of materials, suitable tools, imaginative and role-play, movement, designing and making, and a variety of songs and musical instruments.

Ideas and activities to try

- Create a safe place, perhaps a den, rocker, or nest of cushions for children to watch group role-play and imaginative play, so that they can be close by and observe what is happening.

- Sing simple commentaries that describe the actions of simple pretend play. Model simple pretend play related to the child's everyday experiences, such as bathing dolly, making a phone call and so on, encouraging the child to imitate your actions.

- Try dancing together. Start with gentle quiet music to assess the child's response, then try a wide variety of music. Ask parents what sort of music the child likes at home. Invite other children to join you.

- Look out for textures that the children enjoy. Use these to make a way into other creative activities, such as painting with fur, collage, pretend play brushing furry toys, pegging fur fabric on a washing line.

- Try play people and small world play. Such accurate miniatures are easier for a child to understand.

Top Tips

- Involve parents and siblings in helping the child to develop simple pretend play or role-play.

- Some children are fascinated by characters they see on television or DVDs. Children with Asperger's Syndrome may be powerfully influenced by what they see on DVDs. They enjoy the predictability and repetitiveness, as well as the visual presentation of information. This can be both a benefit and a challenge. Talk with parents about the child's favourite DVDs and plan how these can be used to enhance the child's play and act as a stimulus for other creative activities, perhaps using junk box models to create favourite characters, or recreating scenes in small world or role-play, using the music for dance and so on.

Approaches developed to help children with Asperger's Syndrome

Some key principles and features of each approach

A wealth of research is going on across the globe into possible causes of Asperger's Syndrome and other autistic spectrum disorders. Although it is still far from clear what triggers these disorders and why the prevalence has increased in recent years, this research and the work of many other experts in the field has brought us much closer to understanding the nature of autism and its origins.

This research and also the sharing of expertise and experience has also resulted in a diverse range of approaches to improve the life chances of children and adults with autistic spectrum disorders. Knowing of these approaches is important, as there is much to be learnt that can be adapted and used in the Foundation Stage in early years settings. The list below is far from exhaustive but covers many of the approaches most commonly tried with very young children in the UK.

LOVAAS, or Applied Behaviour Analysis, ABA

What is it?

Developed from the work of Dr Ivar Lovaas, this structured early intervention is a home-based programme delivering up to 40 hours per week of intensive one-to-one teaching, using a structured small steps approach, with a exacting and sophisticated system of reinforcers and rewards.

Key principles:

- a small steps approach;
- highly structured;
- planned reward system;
- learning one to one, by imitation;
- intensive, about 40 hours per week;
- removal of distractions.

> **Find out more from:**
> The Brackens
> London Road
> Ascot, Berkshire, SL5 8BE
> Tel: 01344 882248
> www.peach.org.uk

And for the Early Years Foundation Stage...

Such a small steps structured approach with praise and rewards to increase motivation works well with many children with special needs. Lovaas reminds us that repetition and reinforcement activities need careful planning so that children have plenty of opportunities to practice emerging skills and use newly learnt skills in a range of situations.

What is it?

The Picture Exchange Communications System, first used in the United States, involves the child exchanging a picture of something they want for the actual item. It focuses on providing effective communication for children and in particular on the child initiating the exchange.

Key principles:

- a focused on building effective communication;

- primarily used with children with little or limited speech;

- child initiates the communicative exchange;

- avoids verbal prompts;

- research shows that PECS does not delay speech but promotes its development;

- communication must be clear and purposeful.

And for the Early Years Foundation Stage…

The notion that effective communication needs to be prioritised in the early years and the use of visual prompts is at the heart of effective provision for very young children with Asperger's. PECS' use of simple line drawings to represent an object is a very useful way of building understanding, as well as supporting the explanation of abstract concepts. This approach also provides a useful reminder that communication and interaction skills need to be taught and practiced in real not contrived situations, so that the child needs to initiate the exchange and the purpose of their communication is genuine.

Find out more from:

The National Autistic Society,
393 City Road, London EC1V 1NG   Tel: **020 7833 2299**

Information and training:
www.pecs.com or your local speech and language therapy service

the general autism help line:
0870 600 85 85 www.nat.org.uk

The Son-Rise or Options approach

What is it?

This is an intensive home based approach in which the parents and helpers first join the child in their autistic world and then encourage the child to find different activities and ways of relating. Developed in the US by the parent of a child with autism, this approach stresses the importance of the adults showing complete acceptance of the child and their actions.

Key principles:

- teaches through interactive play;

- uses the child's own motivation;

- involves others joining in with the child's repetitive or ritualistic behaviours;

- places the parent and the child at the centre;

- is non-judgmental and optimistic;

- uses fun, enthusiasm and excitement to motivate the child.

And for the Early Years Foundation Stage...

This focus on social interaction and interactive play will be familiar to early years practitioners. Starting with imitating the child can be a very effective way of beginning early interaction play with very young children with Asperger's. The ability to see repetitive and other stereotypical behaviours as very much a part of the child's Asperger's and a logical response to the confusion and sensory inputs they are feeling is helpful in enabling early years practitioners to manage often difficult behaviours. Son-Rise's emphasis on parents and family can be reflected in the importance of home links with the early years setting and the need to respond consistently to the child at all times, at home and in the early years setting.

Visit the web-site, or look out for the approaches, education and intervention information sheets from the National Autistic Society. They also have a useful article written by a parent of a two-and-a-half year old in an options-based programme. See below for contact details for the National Autistic Society

Find out more from:

The National Autistic Society,
Tel: **0870 600 85 85   www.nas.org.uk**

www.son-rise.org

What is it?

An intervention pioneered by the National Autistic Society, proposing an individual approach based on the needs of the individual. The name describes the approach:

- **S**tructure;

- **P**ositive approaches and expectations;

- **E**mpathy;

- **L**ow arousal;

- **L**inks.

Key principles:

- structure and routines to make the world a safer, more predictable and more easily understood place;

- high but realistic goals and expectations;

- every child is unique and needs an individual approach;

- importance of seeing the world from the child's perspective;

- calm and order reduce stress and anxiety.

And for the Early Years Foundation Stage...

The importance of clear messages, consistent routines and an individual approach, which are central to SPELL, can all be encompassed into a child's individual plan and goals within the Early Years Foundation Stage. It is important to be ambitious and positive for the child, while at the same time ensuring goals are realistic, achievable and measurable. Within busy early years settings, achieving calm can be a challenge! But it is possible to create comfortable, quiet, relaxing areas to which children can retreat when overloaded. This is important for all children, but absolutely vital for children with autistic spectrum disorders.

Find out more from:

The National Autistic Society,
Tel: **0870 600 85 85   www.nas.org.uk**

TEACCH: Treatment and Education of Autistic and related Communication handicapped Children

What is it?

An American programme that uses structured teaching and focuses on the physical environment in which children learn, the individual child's daily timetable, structure and organisation of each activity or task and on the clues and prompts to help the child complete the task.

Key principles:

- highly organised and structured physical environment for learning;
- reducing distractions;
- schedules and timetables are followed rigorously, to order the day;
- work sessions are very focused with a clear structure;
- systematic approach to building skills;
- planned reward systems;
- effective use of prompts to support learning.

And for the Early Years Foundation Stage...

Thinking about the environment and the way it is influencing the child's learning is an important way of tuning into the child's needs. Sometimes, only small changes to the physical setting can make big differences, for example, giving a child a rug to sit on at story time helps to define the space in which they need to stay. A carefully planned small steps approach is most effective in teaching a whole range of early skills, and planning prompts and rewards which take account of the child's learning style, strengths and motivation will ensure the child makes best progress.

Introducing a consistent routine to tasks helps the child to understand what is happening and expected. It reduces anxiety and helps the child to predict what is coming next. A clear and consistent beginning, perhaps a phrase or min-game to start one-to-one sessions works well. End signals are equally important, helping the child to know that the tasks are completed, such as replacing resources in a box, or perhaps folding up the mat. The visual timetables common in TEACCH can be adapted to photo diaries of the day, helping the child to follow the sequence of activities of their day.

> **Find out more from:**
>
> Start at the website of Whinfell School:
>
> **www.whinfellschool.co.uk/autism**
>
> For more information visit
>
> Division TEACCH at **www.teacch.com**

Early Bird approach

What is it?

This is an early intervention programme, developed here in the UK by the National Autistic Society for pre-school children with autism and their parents. It is a three month programme combining group training for parents with individual home visits, and includes video feedback of parents working with their child. The programme is based in South Yorkshire, but there are local programmes in many areas of the country.

Key principles:

- parents are partners in their child's education;

- provides support and encouragement to parents;

- focuses on communication and behaviour;

- develops parents' understanding of autism;

- provides a structure for communication.

And for the Early Years Foundation Stage…

Early Bird's focus on consistency and work with parents will inspire early years practitioners to work creatively with parents to ensure consistency and to provide the best support and encouragement. The focus on communication and social interaction will prompt us to ensure that communication goals are central to individual plans to support children with Asperger's in early years settings.

This approach also emphasises the role of the adult in promoting and structuring communication with the child. Reflecting on and planning the role of the adult in interactions with a child with Asperger's ensures that the child is making the best progress possible.

Find out more from:

NAS EarlyBird Centre
3 Victoria Crescent West,
Barnsley, South Yorkshire
S75 2AE

Tel **01226 779218**
Fax: **01226 771014**
Email: **earlybird@nas.org.uk**

Daily Life Therapy/Higashi

What is it?

The Boston Higashi School provides an international programme of Daily Life Therapy. Developed by Dr Kitahara in Japan, Daily Life Therapy is a holistic approach to the education of children with autistic spectrum disorders, from three years. It is a systematic approach to teaching through group dynamics, modelling and physical activity.

Key principles:

- physical activity and vigorous exercise are used to reduce anxiety, gain stamina and develop rhythm and routines;

- developing physical co-ordination, balance and team work are central;

- art and music are used to develop the child's creativity and appreciation of the arts;

- daily living and social skills are taught as well as other curriculum subjects.

And for the Early Years Foundation Stage…

Physical development is already an important component of the Foundation Stage. The Higashi approach will encourage practitioners to consider the range of physical activities provided and ensure that the co-ordination and balance difficulties many children with Asperger's have are addressed. Working in pairs and small groups is a good way to practice skills, build social skills and reinforce friendships. The Higashi emphasis on self help and independence reminds us of the importance of prioritising these skills and practising them in different situations.

Find out more from:

Visit the website or contact the NAS information line for the information sheet about Higashi and Daily Life Therapy

Auditory Integration training

What is it?

Developed in France by Dr Bérard, an ear, nose and throat specialist, auditory integration training has proved successful with children and adults with hyperacusis, which is over-sensitivity to certain sounds. Treatment involves listening to music, through headphones, which has been modified to their own individual auditory sensitivities and deficiencies.

Key principles:

- bespoke to the individual's needs;

- addresses the child's sensory difficulties;

- helps to reduce stress as the child is better able to manage sensory inputs.

And for the Early Years Foundation Stage...

This approach reminds us of the sensory difficulties encountered by some children with Asperger's. We need to be mindful of these within the setting, ensuring that there are times and places for the child to escape from sensory overload, as well as considering the level of distractions that the child may be experiencing. Read a personal account by a parent at **www.autismfile.com/articles/issue1**

> **Find out more from:**
>
> the auditory integration training organisation at **www.auditoryintegration.net**

Music Therapy

What is it?

Widely accepted as a useful intervention for people with autism as well as people with a diverse range of special needs, music therapy has been available since the 1950s. Provided by highly qualified and specially trained music therapists, music therapy stimulates and develops the use of communication and encourages shared enjoyment and attention, as well as meeting emotional needs.

Key principles:

- includes the most important elements of social interaction;

- helps shared play, turn taking, listening and responding to another person;

- builds tolerance of different sounds and rhythms;

- meets emotional needs.

And for the Early Years Foundation Stage...

The importance of music in the early years is well established, in developing communication, steady beat and understanding of rhythm, for creativity, for expression of feelings and emotions and for shared fun. This approach emphasises how music can be used to meet needs in all areas of learning, and used as a vehicle for building social skills and friendships, as well as for creative expression.

Find out more from:

The British Society for Music Therapy

61 Church Hill Road, East Barnet, Hertfordshire, EN4 8SY

Telephone: **020 8441** 6226   Fax: **020 8441 4118**   **www.bsmt.org.uk**

What is it?

First described by Wendy Prevezer in 1990, musical interaction is a strategy, using singing and percussion instruments, for tuning in to children with autistic spectrum disorders. It uses a balance of active lively play and calmer exchanges to build communicative exchanges between the therapist and the child.

Key principles:

- builds relationship between key worker and the child;

- involves early imitation and surprise games, following a similar pattern to early social play with young babies;

- starts with the child's own sounds and actions, drawing them in gradually to turn taking and imitation;

- allows the child to take the lead;

- includes sung commentaries that describe the child's actions in simple short phrases;

- makes use of and personalises familiar rhymes;

- uses pauses and exaggerated gasps as cues and prompts for the child.

And for the Early Years Foundation Stage…

This approach emphasises the value of simple everyday action rhymes and traditional songs and games. The use of pauses and exaggerated gasps can be most effective in helping the child tune in to the social timing of conversations and play. This fun, child centred, positive approach that is so age appropriate in the Foundation Stage reminds us of the value of music, the importance of social interaction, the crucial role of the key worker and the importance of allowing children to take the lead.

Find out more from:

Read Wendy Prevezer's Strategies for Tuning into Autism on the NAS website, **www.nas.org.uk** or contact the National Autistic Society

Differentiation and reinforcement for children with Asperger's and other autistic spectrum disorders

Understanding differentiation

During the Early Years Foundation Stage, every child will progress at their own pace and each child will have its own unique interests and learning styles. This is, of course, also true for children with Asperger's Syndrome. Children with Asperger's Syndrome generally are of average or above average intelligence, often with a visual learning style and, to a greater or lesser degree, difficulties with communication, social skills and repetitive or narrowly focused interests.

Generally, children with Asperger's learn most effectively when activities are presented with visual clues, planned prompts, meaningful rewards and focus on their very specific learning needs. A systematic small steps approach is often the most effective method, making the most of structures and routine. Like all young children they learn best from doing, from activities focused on everyday situations and routines of particular importance to them. All this may be very much influenced by the child's individual sensory issues. That is the way they perceive and process sensory information and any hypersensitivity to certain sensory inputs, such as hyperacusis (over-sensitivity to certain sounds, such as an audible buzz from light fittings).

Children in the same setting, working alongside each other, can be taught in different ways. This is known as differentiation. Differentiation ensures that teaching is most effective and the child makes the most progress possible. Differentiation is a continuous process, changing in response to the changing needs of the child.

Differentiation involves us in:

- recognising individual needs and learning styles;

- ensuring planned activities are accessible and supplemented to be most effective in meeting the needs of the child;

- observing, assessing and planning; recording and evaluating.

Differentiation can happen in the following ways:

Differentiation by the resources used

This could be using different toys, equipment or materials to make the activity accessible to the child, such as removing the distraction of a particular toy, or by using very simple clear photograph books.

Differentiation by the activity provided

This could be by providing a different but related task, such as matching pairs of everyday objects, instead of matching picture pairs, or a lotto picture game.

Differentiation by group size

This will depend upon the activity, and a child with an autistic spectrum disorder such as Asperger's Syndrome may need one-to-one provision.

Differentiation by the way information is presented

Matching the way instructions and information are provided to the level of understanding, attention and listening skills and learning style of the child. It may also include using clues and prompts, perhaps real concrete objects or other visual prompts such as photographs.

Differentiation by the support provided

Matching the sort of support provided to the needs of the child at that moment. This may be a practitioner working alongside the child in a flexible and responsive way, to supply sensitive intervention or guidance as the child needs it.

Differentiation by the response or outcome expected

This could involve practitioners in expecting and recognising different responses from different children. The child with an ASD might make a pointing gesture rather than verbal response and they might only be able to listen for a short length of time on a particular activity.

The small step, structured approach, using prompts to support learning, provides plenty of opportunity to reinforce skill previously learnt.

Children need to have opportunity to:

- practise emerging skills often;

- use these skills one-to-one and in small groups;

- blend newly learnt skills with existing skills, such as having learnt to match pictures, the child needs to learn to take turns with another child (a previously learnt skill) to match the pictures, building towards playing a small lotto game;

- to have time and opportunity to assimilate their learning and use it spontaneously, in different situations, with different people or independently.

Early years settings are ideally positioned for this, as there are plenty of chances to practice emerging skills as the settings provide:

- a wide range of different activities;

- a flexible approach;

- hands on learning;

- different group sizes;

- opportunity to use all the senses;

- activities using everyday objects and routines.

When working with children with autism, considering differentiation and strategies for einforcing emerging skills is absolutely essential and will make all the difference to everyone involved.

and finally:

Early years practitioners can help develop children's skills by:

- modelling and teaching the child to copy actions;

- using a structured small steps approach;

- developing routines;

- using prompts and clues;

- making the most of physical play and music;

- making rewards meaningful to the child;

- focusing on play to teach communication and social interaction;

- using obsessions and special interests as rewards for attention and achievement.

Who's who in multi-agency working?

Although many children with Asperger's Syndrome in the Early Years Foundation Stage are likely to be still at the stage of assessment, concerns may well have been raised and a range of professionals will be available to offer the child and family support. This team will vary from place to place but is likely to include:

Paediatrician
A hospital or community-based children's doctor, often specialising in children with special needs.

Educational psychologist
Responsible for offering advice and support to schools and for assessing the learning needs of children.

Health Visitor
Working in conjunction with the child's family doctor, providing health advice and support to all parents of babies and young children.

Portage visitor or specialist home teaching
Specialist early years practitioners providing structured learning for babies and young children, often one-to-one in the child's home, and providing advice and support to parents.

Child development assessment centre staff
Either community or hospital-based service providing specialist assessment, diagnosis and ongoing support for babies and young children with special needs and their families

In addition there will be:
Social Services professionals
HomeStart volunteers
Occupational Therapists.

The team may also include parent partnership workers providing independent parental support. In addition, parents may receive advice and support from local or national voluntary organisations, such as local branches of the National Autistic Society.

Early years practitioners include:

setting managers
key workers
Special needs co-ordinator (SENCO)
who ensures the child has the best possible support from the team and an Individual Education or Learning Plan (IEP).

Partnership with parents

The introductory pages of this book will have given you some insight into what it might feel like to be the parent of a young child with Asperger's Syndrome, which is an autistic spectrum disorder. Establishing a good relationship with the parents will bring benefits to you and to them, and ultimately to the child. There is much you (and the parents too) can do to help establish a rapport:

- Make the time to listen to each other.

- Tune into their mood.

- Start and finish on a positive note.

- Ask their opinion.

- Try not to interrupt or say you know just how they feel.

- Let them know how much you enjoy working with their child.

- Find out what they want to know. Some parents particularly want to know what their child has had to eat or drink, what they have being doing, or who they are playing with. Ask them what they need to know.

- Get the message across that you see their child as an individual, not a child with a disorder on the autistic spectrum.

- Mention what you have observed, such as 'I noticed that when I used the Thomas the Tank Engine book, he really concentrated well'.

- Give real positive messages, such as '*name* is really starting to respond to the use of bubbles to mark the end of activities'. Go on to describe the activity and be very specific in your feedback.

- Encourage them to bring in objects and photos from home. Where possible, let them take home particularly helpful resources to borrow, or visit the local toy library together.

- Take account of their priorities when setting targets.

- Work together on planning targets related to self-help skills.

- Be reassuring about meeting their child's toilet needs.

Early years practitioners can help all young children with autistic spectrum disorders by:

- being calm and focused;

- establishing routines;

- being consistent;

- being flexible and open to new ideas;

- always asking themselves 'why?';

- trying to see the world from where the child stands.

Early years practitioners can help parents by:

- making extra time to listen;

- attending multi-agency meetings;

- being positive;

- making the child's targets achievable;

- giving real and regular feedback about what their child has been doing;

- being sensitive to the parent's concerns about their child;

- giving a clear message that you like and respect their child as an individual, seeing them as child first, a child with special needs second.

More ideas

- Put together a photo album of key objects, significant people and favourite toys and activities to share between home and your setting.

- Make a safe place for the child to put special toys or objects they need to bring from home. Make sure both parent and child know it will be safe, but accessible.

- Ask about the rest of the family, such as 'How is *name* with the baby?', or 'What does *name* like doing with his big sister?'

- Talk about what is happening to make inclusion work, such as practical examples of differentiation.

- Ask if you may observe a session when the speech and language therapist, or specialist pre-school teacher is working with the child, so that you can all make sure that you are working together most effectively.

- Make sure the parent has a copy of their child's Individual Education Plan and the targets across all areas of learning.

- If a parent is working or has little time available when they collect their child, do make other arrangements to meet informally to talk, discuss progress and listen to their concerns and aspirations for their child. A home–school diary sheet may help but is no substitute for getting together in person.

Resources and websites

In the Toy Cupboard

Most well-stocked early years settings will have a wealth of resources ideal for meeting the needs of children with Asperger's in the Foundation Stage.

In addition, you might try the local toy library for some of the following:
Photographs of everyday objects, actions and faces with different emotions, check out the catalogue from Speechmark:

Speechmark Publishing Ltd
Telford Road, Bicester, Oxfordshire OX26 4LQ Tel: **01869 244644** Fax: **01869 320040**
www.speechmark.net

For toy libraries visit **www.natl.org.uk**

You could also add the following items to your shopping or 'wish' list:
Sand timers
Plain fabric for distraction-free backgrounds
Plain trays for defining work areas
Scrap and photo books for visual timetables
A camera, instant or digital if possible, but a simple single use camera will do
Wheeled toys for two to ride.

This could also be a good time to review the range of software you have available for the computer – it is such a good medium for presenting information visually, and for activities that need children to work together.

For your bookshelf

SEN Code of Practice on the Identification and Assessment of Pupils with Special Educational Needs (DfES)

Thinking in Pictures
Temple Grandin

The Martian in the Playground
Clare Sainsbury

The Curious Incident of the Dog in the Night Time
Mark Haddon

Asperger's Syndrome - A Guide for Parents and Professionals
Tony Attwood

On the Web

Any search engine will produce hundreds of results for autism and for Asperger's Syndrome. Start your search at the website of the National Autistic Society, at **www.nas.org.uk**.

Also visit autism connect, **www.autismconnect.org** for a worldwide interactive personalised forum and notice board with latest information, research and training. For real insight look for personal accounts of living with autism. Try the work of Temple Grandin and Donna Williams, two very able individuals with autistic spectrum disorders who have written books and articles describing their very personal experiences of autism.

A search on **www.amazon.co.uk** will bring up many titles on autism and Asperger's Syndrome – guides, practical handbooks and individual autobiographies by individuals and their families. There are also lists of popular practitioner handbooks and story books for younger readers about children with autism.

Key Contacts

On the Web:

Start with **www.autismconnect.org** for a worldwide interactive website with a personalised forum and notice board with latest information, research and training. Try also to visit the personal web pages of children and adults with Asperger's and their parents. These are constantly changing but just entering keywords such as 'personal account Asperger's' in any search engine will produce a wealth of results.

Also, try to visit **www.donnawilliams.net** to read about and see the paintings and sculptures of this very talented artist with Asperger's alongside accounts of her early life at home and school.

The National Autistic Society
393 City Road, London EC1V 1NG
Tel: **020 7833 2299**

Autism help line:
Tel: **0870 600 85 85**
www.nat.org.uk

Early Years Support Team based at;
RNI for Deaf people 19-23 Featherstone Street London EC1Y 8SL
www.earlysupport.org.uk